Seashell
PATTERNS Coloring Book

JESSICA MAZURKIEWICZ

DOVER PUBLICATIONS, INC.
Garden City, New York

Note

A perennial favorite for their unique shapes, seashells are among the most popular coloring motifs. This eye-catching collection by artist Jessica Mazurkiewicz features thirty beautiful plates all centered around seashells and other marine life. A delight for colorists of all ages, use pens, pencils, crayons or felt-tip pens to add your own touch to these enchanting illustrations

Bibliographical Note

Seashell Patterns Coloring Book is a new work, first published by
Dover Publications, Inc., in 2011.

International Standard Book Number

ISBN-13: 978-0-486-47559-2
ISBN-10: 0-486-47559-X

Manufactured in the United States by LSC Communications
47559X06   2020
www.doverpublications.com

1

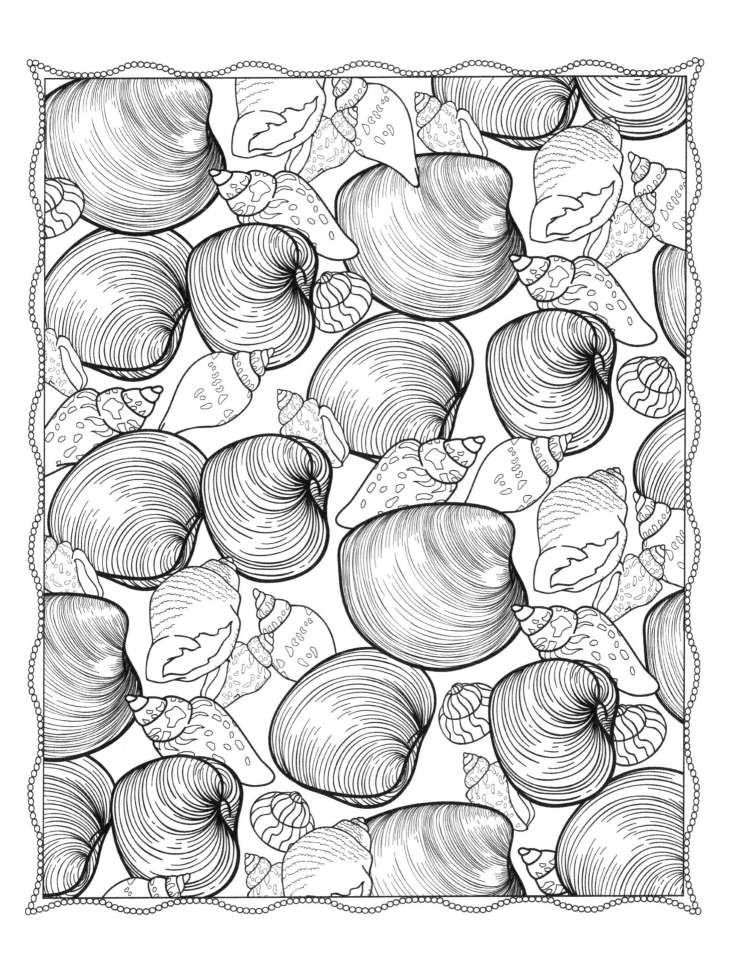

14

16

18